Fredrica McFroodle

Joanna Weaver

Illustrated by Tony Kenyon

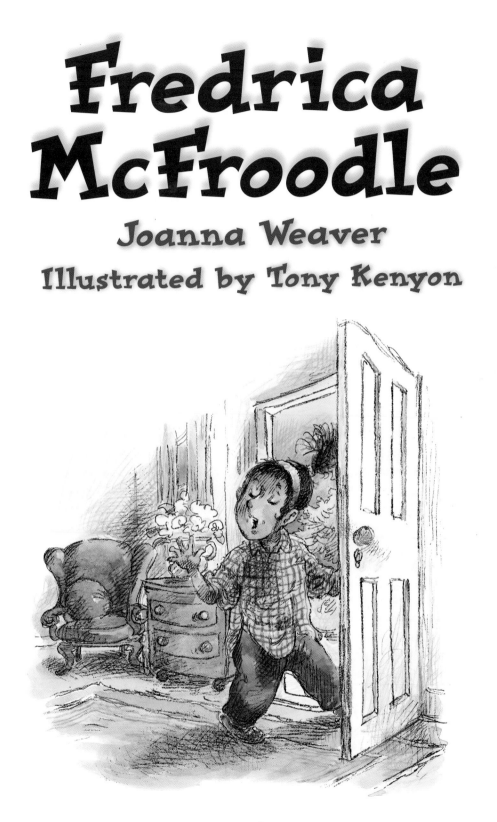

FaithKidz®
Equipping Kids for Life

An Imprint of Cook Communications Ministries • Colorado Springs, CO

Faith Kidz® is an imprint of Cook Communications Ministries,
Colorado Springs, Colorado 80918
Cook Communications, Paris, Ontario
Kingsway Communications, Eastbourne, England

Editor: Kathy Davis
Graphic Design: Granite Design
First printing, 2000
Manufactured in China
04 03   5 4 3 2

Library of Congress Cataloging-in-Publication Data
Weaver, Joanna.
    Fredrica McFroodle / Joanna Weaver ; illustrated by Tony Kenyon.
        p. cm. — (Attitude adjusters)
    Summary: Proud and boastful Fredrica McFroodle suffers defeat in a spelling
bee and asks Jesus to forgive her for her bad attitude.
    ISBN 0-7814-3370-3
    [1. Pride and vanity—Fiction. 2. English language—Spelling—Fiction.
3. Christian life—Fiction. 4. Stories in rhyme.] I. Kenyon, Tony, ill. II. Title.
PZ8.3.W3797 Fr 2000
[E]—dc21
                                                    99-087682

This book belongs to:

_____

"Do not think of yourself more highly than you ought . . ."
Romans 12:3 (NIV)

Fredrica McFroodle

had quite a smart noodle;
she knew all there was to know.
She memorized the Bible
and knew all the tribal
groups down in Ookabungo.

When Fredrica McFroodle
     walked her small poodle
up and down the street,
     with her nose held high,
she walked right by
     people she knew she should greet.

"Why bother?" she said
    with a toss of her head.
"They're not as smart as I . . .
    Can they count to billions
and multiply millions?
    I think not," she said with a sigh.

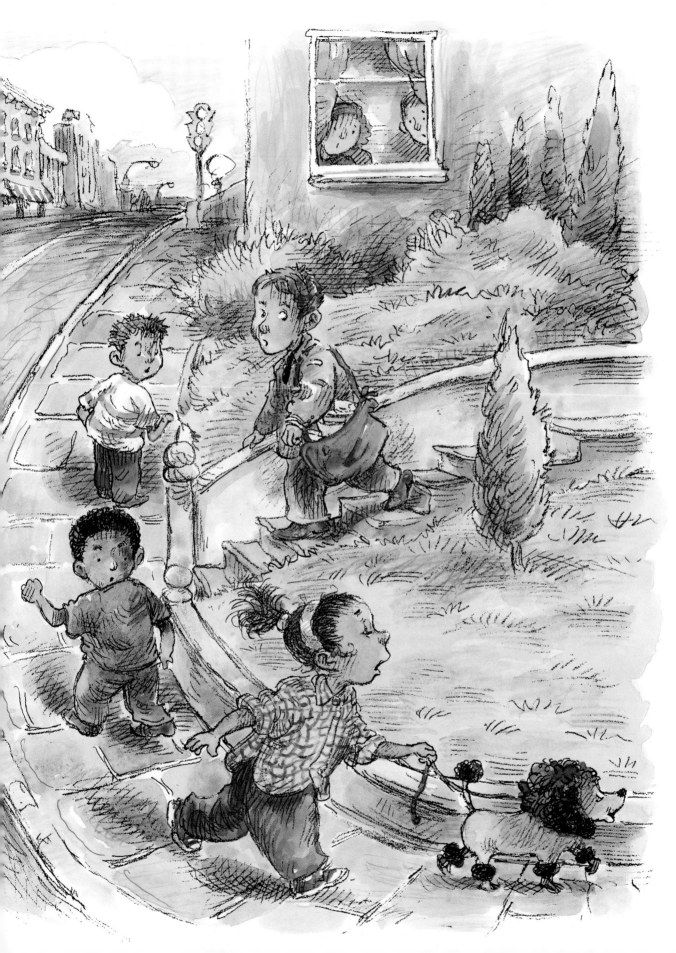

"You sound like a snob,"
	said her little brother Bob
as he listened to big sister boast.

But Fredrica just smiled,
    so sweet and so mild.
"I can't help it if I'm smarter than most."

Fredrica McFroodle had a friend, Polly Doodle.
They played every day after school.
But no matter the game, it was always the same,
Fredrica made up every rule.

"Did you hear Miss Wellingfree
    announce the school spelling bee?"
Polly asked as she played with a doll.
    "I did," said Fredrica,
"I think I shall seek a
    new trophy to place on my wall."

"Well, I practiced last night
    till Mom turned off the light,"
Polly said with her eyes all agleam.
    "I think I did well
because now I can spell
    elevator, perimeter, and scheme."

"That's nice," said her friend,
    "but I don't think I'll spend
much time in study at all!
    My vocabulary's enormous,
with words like *thesaurus*,
    Piccadilly, and *Neanderthal*."

15

That night before bed, the McFroodle family read
    the Bible and had their devotion.
They read Proverbs sixteen, verses one to eighteen,
    and it certainly caused a commotion.

"With pride comes destruction,"
    warned Solomon's instruction.
"And haughtiness leads to a fall."

"Fredrica, watch out!"
    Bobby said with a shout.
"There's no doubt you're
    the proudest of all."

The days flew by fast.
    'Twas the spelling bee at last!
Fredrica took her place on the stage.
    In front of fathers and mothers,
she stood with the others,
    while the teacher read words from a page.

One by one they went 'round,
     till three spellers were found
who knew how to spell every word.
     Fredrica and Polly,
a third-grader named Wally
     remained on the stage undeterred.

"I'm afraid," whispered Polly
    as she watched the boy Wally
spelling the word *delicious*.
    "Do not fear," said her friend.
"Losing isn't the end—
    after all, you're not that ambitious."

But when Wally spelled it wrong,
   Polly had to be strong.
She took a deep breath and she started.
   "D-E-L . . . I-C-I . . ."
Polly sounded so shy,
   "O-U-S?" she asked, fainthearted.

"That's correct!" said Miss Wellingfree.
"This could be the spelling bee!
Are you ready, Fredrica? You're next.
The word is *conceited*.
Do you know it or need a
    definition to help with the text?"

"No, it's really quite easy,"
       she said, bright and breezy.
"C-O-N-S-E-A-T-E-D."
       But instead of applause,
there was silence because
       Fredrica had missed it completely.

23

"Oh, my goodness! Oh, my dear!"
    she cried with a tear.
"That was wrong. Can I try it again?"
    The teacher shook her head,
"I'm so sorry," she said.
        "Rules are rules—page one, section ten."

"Solomon was right,"
    Fredrica said with hindsight.
"Pride really does lead to a fall.
    Dear Jesus, forgive me
and won't You please give me
    a heart that is humble in all."

Fredrica McFroodle's
best friend, Polly Doodle,
took home the trophy that day.
But Fredrica knew why,
and she said with a sigh,
"I'm glad that you won it this way."

"For I was conceited. Forgive me?" she pleaded.
She cried as she hugged her dear friend.
"YOU, Polly Doodle, have quite a smart noodle!"
Then they skipped away happily. The end.

"Do nothing out of selfish ambition or vain conceit, but in humility consider others better than yourselves."
Philippians 2:3 (NIV)

Faith Parenting Guide

Ages: 4-7

Life Issue: I want my child to be humble and put others first.

Spiritual Building Block: Humility

Learning Styles

Sight: Create a "humble pie." Find a used foil pie pan or paper plate. Cut up string to separate the circle into six "slices" of pie. Glue the string down, or draw the divisions with a marker or crayon. In each slice, write one letter of the word H-U-M-B-L-E. Talk with your child about the meaning of the word (thinking of others first, not bragging about yourself, and so on). Then encourage your child to color each slice a different color or even draw a picture in each section of how we can be humble. If you wish, celebrate your time together by eating a real piece of pie!

Sound: Help your child learn the following Scripture passage by heart: "Do nothing out of selfish ambition or vain conceit, but in humility consider others better than yourselves," Philippians 2:3 (NIV). As you work on it together, talk about the meanings of the words *selfish, ambition, vain, conceit,* and *humility.* You may want to look up the words in a dictionary to be sure your child thoroughly understands their meanings.

Touch: What happens when you have too much pride? This object lesson may help your child remember. Using any set of building blocks you have in the house, ask your child to create a "tower of pride." (If you don't have blocks, save up empty cartons and oatmeal and similar containers. Tape up the lids, and you'll have wonderful building tools.) As he or she builds the highest tower possible, talk about what it means to be proud (thinking you are better than others), and how being humble is the opposite. When the tower collapses, point out that being too proud will always result in some kind of downfall. We'll eventually be embarrassed, or sorry, or find we don't have many friends.